T0021676

POCKET STUDY SKILLS

*Series Editor: **Kate Williams**, Oxford Brookes University, UK*
Illustrations by Sallie Godwin

For the time-pushed student, the *Pocket Study Skills* pack a lot of advice into a little book. Each guide focuses on a single crucial aspect of study giving you step-by-step guidance, handy tips and clear advice on how to approach the important areas which will continually be at the core of your studies.

Published

14 Days to Exam Success (2nd edn)
Analyzing a Case Study
Blogs, Wikis, Podcasts and More
Brilliant Writing Tips for Students
Completing Your PhD
Doing Research (2nd edn)
Getting Critical (3rd edn)
How to Analyze Data
Managing Stress
Planning Your Dissertation (2nd edn)
Planning Your Essay (3rd edn)
Planning Your PhD
Posters and Presentations
Reading and Making Notes (2nd edn)

Referencing and Understanding Plagiarism (2nd edn)
Reflective Writing (2nd edn)
Report Writing (2nd edn)
Science Study Skills
Studying with Dyslexia (2nd edn)
Success in Groupwork (2nd edn)
Successful Applications
Time Management
Using Feedback to Boost Your Grades
Where's Your Argument?
Where's Your Evidence?
Writing for University (3rd edn)

POCKET STUDY SKILLS
Peter Hartley, Mark Dawson & Sue Beckingham

SUCCESS IN GROUPWORK

BLOOMSBURY ACADEMIC
LONDON · NEW YORK · OXFORD · NEW DELHI · SYDNEY

BLOOMSBURY ACADEMIC
Bloomsbury Publishing Plc
50 Bedford Square, London, WC1B 3DP, UK
1385 Broadway, New York, NY 10018, USA
29 Earlsfort Terrace, Dublin 2, Ireland

BLOOMSBURY, BLOOMSBURY ACADEMIC and the Diana logo are trademarks of Bloomsbury Publishing Plc

First published in Great Britain 2010
This edition published 2022

A catalogue record for this book is available from the British Library.

A catalog record for this book is available from the Library of Congress.

ISBN: PB: 978-1-3509-3349-1
       ePDF: 978-1-3509-3351-4
       eBook: 978-1-3509-3350-7

Series: Pocket Study Skills

Typeset by Integra Software Services Pvt. Ltd.
Printed and bound in India

To find out more about our authors and books visit www.bloomsbury.com and sign up for our newsletters.

Contents

Acknowledgements vii
Introduction viii

Part 1 Getting ready for groupwork 1

1 Why work in groups at university? 2
2 What do you expect from groupwork? 7
3 The key challenges of groupwork 9
4 What makes groups successful? 12

Part 2 Creating the team 19

5 How groups are selected 20
6 The first meeting: getting it right 24
7 Agree your ground rules 32

Part 3 Organising your group 39

8 Understanding the task 40
9 Team roles 53
10 Organising meetings 62
11 Making decisions 67

Part 4 Relationships and communication 71

12 Analysing what is going on 72
13 Reviewing and revising your ground rules 80
14 Dealing with conflict 92

Part 5 Assessment and reflection 97

15 Meeting assessment criteria 98
16 Reflecting on your experience 102
17 Writing up your reflection 109

Troubleshooting guide 115
References 118
Index 122

Acknowledgements

Our first edition came from the Learn Higher Centre for Excellence, which is now part of the Association for Learning Development in Higher Education (ALDinHE). Many of their resources are useful for students – www.learnhigher.ac.uk.

Thanks to all our former and present (and future) colleagues for their inspiration, support and generosity.

Thanks to our series editor Kate Williams, and to colleagues at Bloomsbury for their support and patience.

We dedicate this book to future generations of students who will find our suggestions useful – especially Jasmine, Jenson, Jackson, Eddie, Alexander, Gregor, Phoebe, Finlay and Sophia. May your groups and teamwork deliver outcomes, outputs and reflections beyond your tutors' expectations.

Introduction

This book offers techniques and ideas you can apply to all the different groups you meet in your course and future career. You can use groupwork on your course to develop skills you need for the future. For example, if you can use online tools to support and enhance face-to-face contact, then you are prepared for whatever becomes your future career.

Many courses include assessed group projects – your grades depend on how your group has worked together. How are you going to make the most of this experience?

Your tutors may expect you to 'get on with it' and not provide much guidance. Even if they do provide support/sessions on groupwork, they cannot be available all the time. But this book can!

All our examples are real student groups from different academic areas who managed groupwork successfully (and a few who did not).

Using this guide

This book will help you prepare, organise and reflect on groupwork. You can read it from cover to cover, or focus on specific areas/issues. We cover the stages and issues you will encounter, offering tips to help you avoid/overcome common pitfalls.

Part 1 Getting ready for groupwork – thinking about your approach to groups/teamwork can help you plan a positive start.

Part 2 Creating the team – the first few meetings are critical to establish the team.

Part 3 Organising your group – planning and organising are often major hurdles, which you can overcome.

Part 4 Relationships and communication – positive group relationships can be achieved through good communication.

Part 5 Assessment and reflection – reviewing your group experience is important for assignments *and* for your future practice.

This book focuses on the most demanding test of group skills – completing a major task in a small group taking several weeks, a semester or even a year. But you can apply our ideas to all groupwork, such as class discussion.

Assignments and reflection

Reflecting on your groupwork experience will help identify the skills you are developing and is often part of assessment. Our theory boxes will help you write up your experience. Specific opportunities to reflect are indicated by the *Hmm …* logo.

Taking it further

For more examples and updates and our documents and checklists, go to: bloomsbury. pub/success-in-groupwork.

PART 1

GETTING READY FOR GROUPWORK

After explaining why student groups are used in higher education, we ask you to think about your expectations before summarising the main benefits of groupwork.

Read this part *before* you start any group project. It will:

- ask what *you* expect to gain from groupwork
- explain the main benefits of groupwork
- summarise the key challenges of groupwork
- introduce key features of successful groups.

Developing valuable skills for your future career

Universities help students develop skills such as 'working with other people' because that is what employers are looking for. The Institute of Student Employers (2018) agrees: 'across the globe, problem solving, the ability to work in a team and communication are considered to be the most important skills'.

Collaboration has always been important – nowadays we also need to work and collaborate effectively online.

You will be asked about your experience of working with others in job/career interviews. Think about yourself from the perspective of a future employer: how many questions from this checklist can you answer now?

Groupwork checklist for job interviews

	Your answer
What experience have you had of teamwork?	
How do you typically behave in groups?	
What was your major contribution to the groups you have worked in?	
What have you learned from your experience in groups?	
How did you help the groups you worked in to sort out any difficulties or conflict?	
What makes groups or teams successful?	
What technology is useful for groupwork?	
Can you give examples of working well with others?	
What is it like to work with teams online?	

Don't worry if you cannot answer all these questions at the moment! This book explains how to achieve successful groupwork, so you *will* be able to answer them.

Improving your learning

Students often report that they learn more from working on a project with other people than they do from individual assignments. They have a 'deeper' or 'richer' learning experience.

Universities and colleges are 'melting pots' – learners come from a wide range of sociocultural and economic backgrounds. You have opportunities to broaden your horizons, meet new people and learn to work effectively with diverse groups. Social scientists highlight the importance of 'cognitive diversity' – bringing together people with different perspectives to develop better solutions to complex problems.

Another important point from social science research: we do not always learn immediately from our experience. We all need to think about (reflect upon) our group experience and decide what went right and wrong – and then decide if we need to behave differently in future. As a starting point, think about how you can apply the model in the Theory box to your own, and your group's, behaviour.

Theory box: Learning through experience

Theory

In the 1970s, David Kolb proposed a theory of 'experiential learning', which describes four key stages: experience, observation, conceptualisation and experimentation (Kolb 1984).

Experiential learning has been hugely influential and can be seen today in the widespread use of approaches like problem-based learning and reflective assignments.

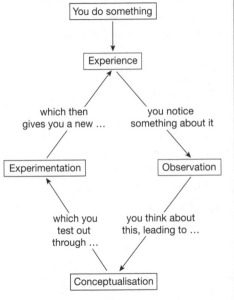

You do something

↓

Experience

which then gives you a new ...

you notice something about it

Experimentation

Observation

which you test out through ...

you think about this, leading to ...

Conceptualisation

Comment

Every theory has limitations, and other academics and practitioners have criticised this approach, suggesting, for example, that it does not take into account the complexity and variety of modern learners.

You can apply Kolb's ideas to your own experience:

For example, you can ask the following questions:

▶ What do you look out for (observation) when you are working in a group?
▶ Do you and your group make time to reflect on what is happening?
▶ Do you try to make sense of what is going on in order to do things differently and achieve more in the future?

Any other thoughts?

In your first class, the tutor is explaining what to expect from the module. You hear the following words: 'and you will be working in small groups from week 3'. Which thought bubbles are closest to your reaction?

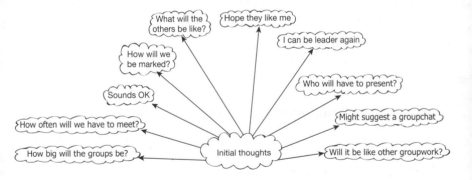

Most students have mixed expectations about working in groups. On the positive side, you can look forward to developing new relationships and achieving more than you could on your own. On the negative side, you may worry about whether the members will get along or be able to work well together.

These concerns are very common. For example, Beeson and Byles (2020) found that their students had experienced *all* the specific problems covered in this guide; the most common were lack of availability for meetings, communication, different levels of contribution in the group, and personality clashes. Beeson (2021) has also produced useful practical guidance.

Unfortunately, there is no 'magic formula' for group success, no one best way of organising your group. You have to think about and adapt our ideas and suggestions to your own situation.

Looking beyond your immediate group

If you are feeling uncertain about working in groups, remember that great advances and accomplishments increasingly come from teams – they can achieve bigger and better things (Syed 2019). For example, many successful startup companies and social enterprises came from a small group (often students) who spotted an opportunity and decided to run with it.

Working effectively with other people takes a bit of getting used to. It is a valuable skill. Like any skill, you get better at it with practice.

The main challenges you will face on group projects tend to fall into three main categories: communication, organisation and workload.

Communication and relationships

Group members have to work together as a team (you do not have to like everybody, though) and keep each other informed about important developments.

Effective communication doesn't just mean that people understand you. You also need to understand everybody. Each group member needs to feel confident that their thoughts will be listened to and considered fairly. Many problems faced by groups are a result of poor (or complete lack of) communication.

As a group, you need to decide which online tools you are going to use to communicate. These might include chat tools for quick messages, meeting tools for planning and collaborative tools to produce the work.

Organisation

Often, groups run into difficulties because they have not organised sufficiently. Make sure you avoid the common pitfalls. Groups can fail if they:

▶ lose sight of their common purpose
▶ do not know who is supposed to be doing what and by when
▶ do not meet regularly and/or communicate
▶ create multiple versions of documents, which quickly generates confusion.

Technologies such as online communication and collaborative documents offer useful benefits here, as we explain later.

Workload

Group members have to agree to (and complete) a fair share of the workload. One common complaint from student groups is that some members are not participating or contributing enough to the project.

At the very least, these three issues cause inconvenience and result in more stress and a less successful project. At worst, a complete breakdown in communication can mean a failed project.

Most of our suggestions relate to one or more of these issues, so it is worth regularly reviewing these fundamental questions. Try this simple checklist to monitor how you are doing and make notes – **remember you may need to write this up for a reflective assignment**.

Key issues checklist

	Check	Evidence/examples
Are we communicating effectively? • In person/meetings? • Online? • Via chat or texts?		
Are we well organised? • Regular meetings? • Actions recorded? • Updates/reflections?		
Are we sharing the workload? • Is everyone contributing? • Are the actions fair?		

What makes groups successful?

Searching Google with this question produces over 1,250,000,000 results. DuckDuckGo, another search engine, generates similar numbers but *different* top results. This huge number of results reflects the fact that no one 'magic formula' can guarantee success.

Tip: Always use more than one search engine when looking for important resources.

Within this advice, some success characteristics are regularly repeated, although researchers may describe them in slightly different ways. For example, the Harvard Business School publication *Teams that click* (2004) is often quoted as a useful guide. It suggests 'three essentials of an effective team': commitment, competence and a common goal. The theory box includes a word cloud of common factors from other studies of groups.

Our advice focuses on these 'top factors' – your team should demonstrate as many as possible. For example, is everyone in the group committed to the group goals?

Theory box: Recipes for effective teams

Social scientists and analysts often distinguish between 'groups' – a collection of people who are together in some sense – and 'teams' – a collection of people who have a shared purpose and feel some commitment to each other.

The important issue (for theory and practice) is how 'groups' become 'teams'. Another way of expressing this is to say that groups must become teams so they can be effective.

Studies of effective teams have highlighted several factors, shown in the word cloud.

One point to remember: a lot of research on groups was done some years ago, when groups made much less use of online tools and collaboration than we see today. When you look for studies to help your reflections and comparisons, try to find ones that have a similar context to your situation.

Michael West, a leading UK researcher, offers proposals for effective team development that can be applied to both face-to-face and online collaboration. For example, he argues that effective teams should actively and regularly reflect on the way they are setting about their tasks and how members are supported socially, e.g. resolving conflict or interpersonal tensions. You can find a useful questionnaire to test your 'team reflexivity' in his book (West 2012).

In your experience of working in groups, what have been the most important factors in their success?

▶ How do they relate to the factors identified by social scientists?
▶ Can you compare the experience of your present group(s) with accounts from research studies or business case studies? What can you learn from this comparison?

∘ ○ ∘

Reflecting on your group experience

If you have to complete a reflective assignment, look for recent research on group/team development – and use the questions in the theory box to make notes.

Comparing research findings with your own experience is a great way to approach reflective work. But remember, these groups may not operate in the same way as your student group. For example, in organisations, the hierarchy is always influential – a 'boss' is formally responsible for the group. This is obviously not the norm in your student groups – you have to work out your own structure. This means that every member should contribute and take responsibility.

Developing your recipe for success

Although there is no one perfect recipe, your group can develop a successful process by working through all the sections in this book and discussing them. Adapt our suggestions to your own context.

Some characteristics may be especially important for your group in your situation. For example, after surveying over 180 working teams over three years, Google found two features that distinguished successful from less successful teams (Coding Tech 2018):

'High average social sensitivity': Members were above average in the way they recognised and acted on the feelings of the other members.

Equality of communication: In successful teams, everyone contributed equally.

And finally

Communication is critical as it underpins everything you do.

Effective communication supports your tasks, and can develop an inclusive team where everyone is valued and encouraged to contribute to the best of their ability. Every individual is unique, and dimensions of diversity (including race, ethnicity, gender, sexual orientation, socioeconomic status, age, physical abilities and neurodiversity) provide new perspectives that we can all learn from.

Communication in teams

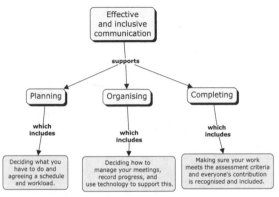

The key issues we look at later in this book include:

▶ What will your plan look like?
▶ How are you going to organise?
▶ Do you know what you are trying to achieve?
▶ How can you ensure that all team members feel valued and respected?

Reflecting on your experience, and how you adapt your communication to work with new colleagues, will help you develop essential teamwork skills.

CREATING THE TEAM

Part 2 examines ways to help the group start to become an effective team. It looks at:

▶ how groups are selected

▶ how to get the first meeting right

▶ how to agree your ground rules.

5 How groups are selected

Tutors can use three ways to select groups:

1 Random allocation, like counting off people where they are sitting, 1, 2, 3 … 6.
2 Letting students choose themselves.
3 Using specific criteria to form the groups.

Each method has advantages and disadvantages, and suggests a slightly different approach in your first meeting.

What approaches have you experienced? What were their pros and cons?

Random allocation

If your group is chosen randomly, the mix of abilities and temperaments should be random. This can be useful – the group can generate a variety of different ideas. On the other hand, there is higher risk of conflict due to personal differences. Make sure you spend enough time getting to know the other members and identify the skills that different individuals bring to the group.

Choosing your own group

Choosing your own group sounds attractive, but beware possible pitfalls. Your friends are likely to be similar in outlook and attitudes, providing only a limited range of opinions. On the other hand, working with people you know already can help the group start quickly.

In this situation, think carefully about choosing other members. Which combination of your friends is most likely to be successful? Ensure that you set your ground rules – this can help friends to be more professional.

Tutor allocation

Tutors often allocate students to groups to achieve a mix, taking into account gender, experience, cultural backgrounds or other criteria. Spend time checking everyone is clear on the task – people might have quite different ideas.

Theory box: How should groups be selected?

Theory

Organisations pay increasing attention to the ways they set up/support working groups so they have the right mix of social and technical skills (Coyle 2018).

Growing research evidence suggests that some characteristics of groups are important. For example, Wheelan (2009) found work groups with three to six members were both more productive and more developed (see pp. 102–3) than groups with seven or more.

One study demonstrated that self-selected student groups were more likely to perform better *only if* their members had taken account of certain factors, like individual skills and knowledge, ability to manage tasks and likely social cohesion, when they formed (Seethamraju and Borman 2009).

Comment

More research on student groups is needed so that we know which findings can be generalised, especially as other research has found major differences between different groups (Chiocchio and Essiembre 2009).

Remember our advice from Part 1 – always look at the context for any academic research you review. Look for similarities and differences with your own experience.

How has your group been selected?

▶ What might be an advantage for your group?
▶ What might be a disadvantage?
▶ What does this mean for how you are going to operate?

∘ ○ ∘

Making a positive start

The first meeting is critical – it can create a positive atmosphere with lasting impact. It may be the first time you have met at least some of the other members. Even if you know the others, it may be the first time you have worked on the same project. In either case, the first meeting is where you get to know each other and start organising the rest of the project. Getting it right can give you a big push on the way to success.

Be positive

Approach the meeting with a positive mindset, open to the idea of working with other people, or you run the risk of appearing negative to others.

Positive behaviours encourage discussion and cooperation. Negative behaviours act like a brake, preventing the group from moving forward in discussion. Even just one person who is consistently positive can have an important impact on the group – encouraging other members to contribute.

Positive behaviours encourage discussion and cooperation. How many do you use in a new group situation?

Behaviours that appear positive	Behaviours that can appear negative
Smiling	Frowning or looking bored
Facing the group	Not facing the group
Asking questions	Saying very little or nothing
Offering suggestions	Criticising others' ideas
Taking relevant notes	Getting distracted by personal texts/notifications
Talking mostly about the project	Talking mostly about irrelevant and non-project stuff

Hmm...

Do you have a positive mindset about groupwork? Think about what you might get out of the group project:

▸ What general skills might you learn?
▸ What might you learn about the subject?
▸ What might you learn about working with others?
▸ What might you learn about yourself?

Meeting places

Your first face-to-face meeting may have to be in the teaching room – a tiered lecture theatre makes that difficult. Make the effort to move or turn your chairs around, so you are talking in a group, not sitting in a row!

Your first meeting may be online. You might use video chat or breakout rooms. Turning on both camera and audio helps to establish a positive atmosphere – and remember to mute the microphone when you are not speaking.

Whatever system you use, try to apply the positive behaviours mentioned above.

During a longer project, you may want to use more than one online meeting system to see the differences and provide useful experience to talk about in future job interviews.

Some useful tips for online meetings:

▸ Upload a profile image. Blank profiles can seem impersonal. You may not always be able to use your webcam if the network signal is weak. Choose your image wisely. A friendly image is usually best.
▸ Use live video chat for main meetings. This allows longer discussions to happen more efficiently.
▸ Some people find it easier if video is not on. Although this makes it difficult to pick up important facial cues, it can help people to listen rather than focus on the images.

- Use the 'hands-up' feature to indicate someone wants to speak. This can help prevent people talking over each other.
- Online communication (especially on messaging applications) can encourage people to be more open, but it is important to set some ground rules (see section below).

And remember, if you plan an online meeting, make sure everyone gets the link.

Getting to know people

You need to find a conversation starter that helps you exchange information, which members of the group will not find intrusive or embarrassing. This can help group members' self-confidence and establish a positive working atmosphere.

Possible starting points include:

- Have you ever done anything like this project before?
- Do you have any previous experience of groupwork? Any good suggestions for making it work well?
- What interests have we got in common?
- Let's organise a group chat. What software should we use?

How might you introduce yourself to a group for the first time?

▶ Is there something you could use to identify yourself uniquely?
▶ What are your likes/dislikes about groupwork?
▶ What are your strengths/weaknesses?

Example

In the first session of a first-year module, each small group of Engineering students was asked to produce their groupwork ground rules. One member of the group set up a Google Doc and invited members of the group to use it. This document was then used by everyone to suggest and comment on ground rules.

To break the ice, they started trying to find something they had in common. They discovered a shared passion for a particular brand of motorbike and became a strong, cohesive group – supporting each other all the way through the three-year course.

Taking time

You may not instantly like all the other members of the group. This is another reason for taking time to get to know the other members. You may also want to reflect on where your negative impressions have come from.

Can you think of a time when you weren't sure about someone at first, but you grew to quite like them?

▶ Why were you not sure at first?
▶ What won you over?
▶ How might being mindful of this example, and any other similar experience, affect how you approach groupwork?

Your technology map

One important advantage you have is the range of technologies to support your groupwork. This includes university/college systems such as the virtual learning environment (VLE; e.g. Blackboard, Moodle or Canvas), plus the apps/software on laptops, tablets and/or smartphones. You need to decide which technologies to use.

Universities and colleges have different systems. Your tutors will share information about their modules through the VLE. This may include facilities your group can use, such as wikis, blogs and/or discussion boards. Your institution may also have systems such as Microsoft Teams for groupwork. These support all or most of the tasks listed in the table below.

Before you decide on which technology to use, make time to check what is available and discuss what will help you make progress. For example, if you rely on university systems, will everyone in the group have equal access to these off-campus? Use the following table as a starting point. As software and apps are changing so fast, you can find a more detailed version on the website.

What you must do	University systems?	Personal systems/apps?	Things to think about
Keep in touch	Email	Email Texting Messaging Group chat	Which system will everyone use regularly?
Generate ideas	Concept and mind mapping	Concept and mind mapping. Word clouds e.g. Wordle	Is everyone used to this kind of software?

What you must do	University systems?	Personal systems/ apps?	Things to think about
Plan and schedule	MS Project Google Sheets	Project planners, e.g. Trello, Zoho	Which app is easiest to use and share?
Research information	Library tools and facilities, e.g. Google Scholar	Online search tools, e.g. Mendeley	Which tools work best for your subject area?
Storing and editing documents	Personal or group file storage	Cloud storage, e.g. DropBox	What do you need to keep long term after the project – which system is best for this?
Meeting	Online conferencing, e.g. in Teams	Online meeting apps, e.g. Zoom or Skype	Which system is most accessible and reliable in your context?
Producing visual aids	Visio (in Microsoft Office)	Infographics Concept/mind maps, e.g. Cmap	Which form of presentation is best for your key messages?
Assembling your final presentation	Presentation software, e.g. PowerPoint	Prezi, Keynote, or concept mapping with presentation facilities, e.g. Cmap	What will you have to produce for assessment?

A good way to get your group off to a good start is to agree guidelines or ground rules to ensure that everyone is clear from the start about what is expected.

Ground rules can be divided roughly into two categories:

1 Communication and attitudes: how group members behave towards one another.
2 Working practice: group procedures and organisation.

Students' first thoughts about ground rules tend to focus on general aspects of communication, such as:

- treating everyone with respect and dignity
- giving everyone an equal opportunity to voice their ideas and opinions
- keeping others informed of anything that might affect the project, e.g. personal issues
- being professional and responsible.

Expressed like this, 'rules' do not necessarily translate easily into specific behaviour; for example, what do you understand by 'respect'? You might say something you see as 'respectful', but others see as a 'microaggression' (see p.85).

So, try to give examples of how you want the group to behave and use something like the suggestions below to record your responses.

Example ground rules for communication and attitudes

Agreed principle	How we are going to do this
Treating everyone with respect and dignity	Use positive body language Give everyone a chance to speak Be polite to one another Listen and pay attention to each other Acknowledge other members' opinions

Example ground rules for working practice

Area of practice	What we agreed
When and where will the team meet?	Regular weekly meeting after the class.
Behave professionally	Turn up on time for meetings. No one should be more than 10 minutes late without sending a message to the rest of the group.

Area of practice	What we agreed
Will there be team or meeting roles?	Need to have someone take notes at each meeting. Everyone takes a turn at this.
How will we decide things?	Aim for consensus and only use voting as a last resort.

Other useful areas for ground rules include: how you are going to allocate work; what happens if someone is ill; and what happens if someone doesn't do what they said they would.

Make sure everyone contributes to this shared document. Also, ensure that someone writes up what you have agreed and emails it round (or posts a shared document) so there can be no vagueness about what was said.

Review your ground rules from time to time to make sure they are working as you intended. If they are not, make changes – and again, write down and circulate a single, agreed version. Consider sending a copy to your tutor and discussing it with them if there is any tutorial time.

Online communication

Online group communication can be very different from face-to-face communication – see the theory box on p. 36. People are often much more open and informal when they use messaging applications, and it may be worth considering some general rules for this too. Check out these 'netiquette' rules for some guidance:

USING CAPS IS LIKE SHOUTING – USE WITH CAUTION!

- ▶ Be careful if you use sarcasm – it can seem much harsher online.
- ▶ Don't overuse emoticons, GIFs, images and videos – stay on topic.
- ▶ Don't create subgroups that exclude group members.
- ▶ Be polite when asking people to do things.
- ▶ Try to contribute to conversations.
- ▶ Do answer people, especially if you are directly addressed.
- ▶ If disagreement starts to get heated, consider pausing the discussion until you can meet in person. Usually, conflict is best resolved face to face.

Theory box: Understanding online communication

Online communication is not the same as face to face: the most obvious difference is the difficulty in seeing/interpreting others' nonverbal behaviour. It can be more tiring – needing extra concentration – one reason for keeping online meetings short and well organised. Bailenson (2021) identifies four causes for 'Zoom fatigue':

▶ excessive amounts of close-up eye contact is 'highly intense'
▶ seeing yourself all the time is fatiguing
▶ sitting all the time reduces our mobility
▶ online conferencing is more demanding, it creates higher 'cognitive load'.

Bailenson makes a number of suggestions to resolve the problems:

▶ reduce the window on screen so you do not see others as very large images
▶ hide or minimise the view of yourself
▶ restructure your space, e.g. use external webcam and keyboard so you are not 'tethered' to the laptop
▶ make time for audio-only breaks, or use screen share so that everyone has something to look at which is not themselves.

∘ ⊙ ∘

And so to the task

Taking a bit of time to get to know your team and establish ground rules helps avoid problems often caused when groups rush straight into detailed task planning. By making the effort to create a *team* spirit, your group will be well prepared to move on to thinking carefully about the task and how to organise yourselves to achieve it!

Beware of rushing into detailed planning before you are sure that everybody agrees the group priorities. You will need to deal with any anxieties from members who 'just want to get on with it'. Their ideas may not be shared by other members and may not be the most effective approach.

Part 3 examines different ways of interpreting the task and planning actions.

ORGANISING YOUR GROUP

Part 3 suggests ways of organising your group to make the most effective use of your time. It includes the following issues:

▶ understanding the task

▶ considering team roles

▶ organising meetings

▶ making decisions.

8 Understanding the task

People often interpret instructions and tasks in different ways. Do not leap into specific activities before you are confident that all group members share a common view of what you are trying to achieve.

Think about how you might approach the following three tasks before you read our analysis. What are the most important things you need to decide and prepare for?

Task A: for first-year Computing students

Select one of these topics: *Artificial intelligence and robotics* or *Big data analytics* or *Cybersecurity*. Present a poster that highlights latest developments in that area. Produce an accompanying fact sheet (not more than one side of A4).

Task B: for second-year Psychology students

Pupils in a class at a local secondary school are anxious about public speaking and presentations. Give them a 15-minute presentation on how to combat nerves, based on relevant psychological research and theory.

Study water pollution along the course of a local stream/river. Write up your research as a scientific report for the council's Environmental Health Department and deliver a 20-minute presentation to members of the local council.

What do you have to do?

Look at the tutor's instructions very carefully. Make sure you agree on what is required (and by when). Make sure you have details of all the practical requirements, e.g. time for any presentation, rules on format etc.

In the three examples above, there are important differences between the tasks. For example:

▸ **Different formats have different rules:** There are specific rules and conventions for scientific reports but not always for posters or presentations.
▸ **Your audiences are very different:** In A, the audience isn't stated so you might have some flexibility for your design and language. In B, ensure your language/design is appropriate for schoolchildren. In C, you need to be professional and recognise that your audience are not subject experts.

▶ **What you research and how you use this research are different for each project**: In A, you need to summarise the latest research and professional practices. In B, you need to work out how to *apply* the relevant research in a practical way. In C, you will be conducting your own research, using previous studies to guide you.

You may not find all the information you need in the assignment brief:

▶ Tutors may deliberately leave things open so that you have freedom of choice. For example, you may have been given a broad subject area and you must decide what subtopic to focus on.
▶ If in doubt, ask. Tutors sometimes make mistakes and forget to include details.

To make sure you have covered everything, discuss with your group and combine your ideas in a shared document. Use the table below to rephrase the tutor's instructions in your own words.

When you have enough experience of presentations in your subject, you can tailor this table to your context.

Understanding the assignment checklist

Key question	Your response
What do you think the project is about?	
What is the tutor expecting you to do?	
What does the assessment involve? You need to decide what the assessment methods involve and how to prepare for them, e.g. will there be any peer and self-assessment, or individual reflective piece to write?	
What will the tutor think is a 'good' project? What are the assessment criteria? How will the tutor distribute marks, e.g. will there be separate marks for content, format, presentation, or referencing? Look at the assessment criteria for the top marks to work out the key qualities.	
What sort of 'audience' will the tutors be when they receive your presentation and grade your assignment? For example, will they be acting as experts or will they be trying to judge how you communicate to a non-expert audience?	

Example assignment checklist for Task A

Key question	Your response
What do you think the project is about?	We need to decide important developments in cybersecurity. But we cannot cover everything – how do we decide what is really important? Can we focus on one particular organisation – need to check this with tutor.
What is the tutor expecting you to do?	Library and internet research: make sure we cover the latest publications on the web (e.g. blog posts by leading international security experts) and in print formats (e.g. professional and trade journals). We can earn extra credit by talking to people in the industry. How can we contact them? How can we explain to them what we want to discuss?

Key question	Your response
What does the assessment involve?	Poster and fact sheet. We need to check: format of the poster (size, orientation, etc.) Delivery platform (might the tutor ask us to present online?) How long will we be asked questions? Are there any format requirements for the fact sheet?

Key question	Your response
How should we organise our answers?	Our poster will look at cybersecurity in three areas – phishing, denial of service and virus attacks – and then present some general conclusions. Our fact sheet will include examples and weblinks.

Key question	Your response
What will the tutor think is a 'good' project?	Tutor checklist for the assessment criteria includes: quality of research; critical analysis; and quality of presentation.
What are the assessment criteria and learning outcomes?	The assignment asks us to: produce accurate information showing that we have done the necessary research; produce conclusions we can back up. The poster and fact sheet must summarise our main argument and contain the most important information. They must be well presented and easy to understand. We must be ready to answer questions on the poster.
What sort of 'audience' will the tutors be?	Tutors will be asking us questions about the poster and fact sheet. They will be in their tutor role and so we can use technical terms and assume they know how the technology works.

Examples

Groups of first-year Psychology students had to find an important and recent study of group behaviour *and* explain how it related to their own experience of coming to university. Several groups found interesting studies and did lots of background reading, but their presentations did not explicitly consider how the work related to *their own experience* – they failed to address one of the main assessment criteria. As a result, their presentations were graded lower than those groups who read the assessment brief more carefully.

Groups of first-year Media students had to edit a short podcast from the tutor, which included many errors (pauses, slips of the tongue, 'ums' etc.). All the groups except one edited out the errors. One group did more complicated edits, which made the tutor's speech much worse (and very funny). Their accompanying notes showed clearly how their edits met the assessment criteria (e.g. technical quality) – and received top marks. So, you can be successful by thinking creatively about the task: just make sure you have the confidence and detailed preparation to carry it off.

Generating ideas

Once everyone is clear about the task, the group can start discussing ideas about how to proceed. How do we find out people's initial thoughts?

There are a number of ways of doing this. For example:

1 **An organised brainstorm in 'real' time:** Allow time for thinking and give everyone space to write their ideas where everyone can see them, e.g. on a physical board using 'sticky' notes, on a whiteboard, or on flipchart paper. Do not start any discussion until everyone has had a chance to contribute all their ideas.

2 **Online brainstorm:** You can use a chat application or a virtual whiteboard like Trello or Padlet using virtual 'sticky' notes.

3 **A group homework/research task with a deadline:** You can use online methods like chat applications and virtual boards to do this too, asking everyone to contribute by a certain date and time. An advantage of doing this over time rather than 'live' is that it helps people who benefit from extra time and space to come up with ideas. You might have non-native English speakers in your group, or group members who are very shy. People are often much more willing to give ideas if they have time to think about them first!

4 **Use concept mapping:** An example concept map with some initial ideas for Task A is shown opposite. These ideas can be expanded into an overall plan. We used Microsoft Visio to produce this map. If you do not have access to this or similar software, we recommend Cmap. The software is freely available at https://cmap.ihmc.us.

Making your plan

A good plan does not have to be a complicated document. It does need to be agreed and shared, and it should have clear targets and deadlines.

Milestones

Identify the key targets that have to be achieved at particular stages – often called 'milestones'. They determine how you need to organise your time. Start from the final deadline and work back. An example outline plan for a group doing Task A is on p.50.

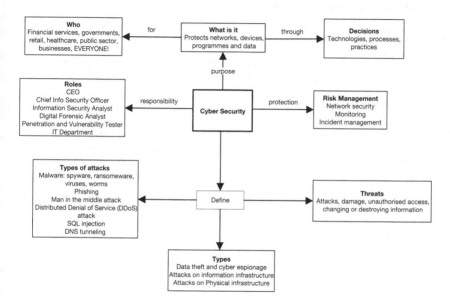

Who
Financial services, governments, retail, healthcare, public sector, businesses, EVERYONE!

for

What is it
Protects networks, devices, programmes and data

through

Decisions
Technologies, processes, practices

purpose

Roles
CEO
Chief Info Security Officer
Information Security Analyst
Digital Forensic Analyst
Penetration and Vulnerability Tester
IT Department

responsibility

Cyber Security

protection

Risk Management
Network security
Monitoring
Incident management

Types of attacks
Malware: spyware, ransomeware, viruses, worms
Phishing
Man in the middle attack
Distributed Denial of Service (DDoS) attack
SQL injection
DNS tunneling

Define

Threats
Attacks, damage, unauthorised access, changing or destroying information

Types
Data theft and cyber espionage
Attacks on information infrastructure
Attacks on Physical infrastructure

Example project plan for Task A

Wk	Need to do	Project milestones
1	*Meeting 1* Make introductions and agree ground rules Agree where/how you will communicate Agree where you will store documents Share initial ideas on project	Share contact information Agree ground rules Decide on technologies
2	*Meeting 2* Agree details of topic – cybersecurity Agree approach/focus, e.g. areas/issues Allocate individuals to areas	Agree on topic Agree approach and methods Delegate members to specific areas to research
3	*Meeting 3* Discuss research so far Decide what further work is needed	Review of research
4	*Meetings 4 and 5* Compare results of research in three areas Discuss overall format of presentation Decide on extra materials (handouts) Review action plan	Complete research Decide conclusions Agree presentation format

Wk	Need to do	Project milestones
6	*Meetings 6 and 7* Compile final presentation and handouts Final rehearsal of the presentation	Agree and rehearse final presentation

Before you finalise your plan, do a reality check. For example, this plan only leaves two weeks to do the research – is this enough? What if you decide to contact some people in organisations to talk to – are you confident that you will be able to find the right contact and arrange a meeting at such short notice?

Can you give everyone a fair share of the workload? For example, if you have five members and three areas to research, how do you allocate tasks?

Have you given yourself enough time to rehearse and polish the presentation?

Reality checklist

	OK?
Does this timescale fit in with group members' existing commitments? Will everyone be able to get to all the meetings?	
Does this plan give you the basis for a fair distribution of the workload?	
Are your timescales realistic? Allow extra time to take account of slippage, delays and the unexpected.	

9 Team roles

Some groups decide that the best way to organise themselves is to allocate certain roles. Team roles often include a leader/manager – but beware of adopting styles that will only work in organisations with a clear hierarchy.

Other roles that student groups often develop include chair, note-taker, researcher, designer, etc. Having set roles can make it easier to allocate tasks but can also be a source of conflict, as some roles are perceived to have more responsibility or volume of work than others. And some roles may be seen as higher status, causing resentment from other team members.

Theory box: Leadership vs. management

Theory

Some theorists distinguish between 'leadership' skills (making sure the group is going in a clear direction, especially in change situations) and 'management' skills (making sure the group is well organised and productive – the preferred style for situations of 'stability'). Being a leader or manager is often seen as mutually exclusive: you are either one or the other. More recent research challenges these views. For example, Azad et al. (2017) argue that effective leaders must be able to manage and effective managers must be able to lead – they need to deploy different styles at different times to ensure continued team success.

Comment

Most research on leadership and management looks at groups in organisations, not in education. In student groups, a team leader/manager has to be more of a 'facilitator' rather than someone who gives orders or instructions. They have to use their persuasive skills to ensure good communication, organised and fair working, and a positive team climate.

Often teams choose to have less strict team roles but may decide to have certain roles in meeting situations. These can be rotated to ensure fairness.

Another useful approach is to look at the behaviours that team members demonstrate in successful groups. For example, Leskinen et al. (2020) found four 'leadership moves' that made important contributions to groups: coordinating group activity; exploring new ideas; seeking out resources; and offering guidance and support to other members.

Do you see yourself as having particular leadership and management skills?

▸ If so, how would you describe these? And how successful are they?
▸ Are there areas you would like to improve?

∘ ○ ∘

Deciding group roles

Good leadership can keep a group focused and motivated, ensuring that things move forward by deciding things quickly. This does not mean that one person has to 'be leader'. Groups can organise in different ways and be equally effective. You need to agree ways of working to suit your mix of personalities and complete the task. That is why it is so useful for the group to discuss how you are going to do things.

Many teams decide not to have an overall leader but instead have someone to lead or 'chair' the team meetings. This role can be rotated or shared to ensure that more than one team member gets the chance to do this and that responsibility is shared. You can also rotate or share the roles in the following table – allowing members to develop different skills. Rotation also helps since some roles are more popular than others.

There are many different ways of organising group roles and one practical suggestion is on the following page. Also consider some of the research on group roles, as in the next theory box.

Possible group roles

Role	Description
Facilitator/chair	Directs the discussion. Tries to ensure that the meeting is productive.
Note-taker	Prepares an agenda for the meeting and shares it. Makes (and shares) notes of the key discussion points, decisions and actions.
Timekeeper	Ensures the team keeps to deadlines.
Resource manager	Makes sure that all the technology is working OK and everyone has access to all group documents/resources.
Critic	Tries to spot flaws in the group's plans and suggest alternatives. (This can be a difficult role so should be rotated between members.)

Theory box: Team roles

Theory

One popular theory of team roles was developed by Meredith Belbin, using his research on management teams (Belbin 2010). Using ideas of intrinsic personality traits, Belbin devised a self-diagnostic tool to assess the roles that individuals are most likely to adopt in groups.

He defines nine roles, which all make a positive contribution to an effective team. We summarise eight, the most important ones for student groups.

Belbin's team roles

Role	Someone effective in this role will be good at ...
Implementer	getting things done and focusing on practical issues
Coordinator	organising the task and other members of the group
Shaper	inspiring and leading the group from the front
Plant	generating ideas and being creative
Resource investigator	identifying resources that can help, which may be outside the group
Monitor evaluator	evaluating ideas/proposals; pointing out possible flaws
Team worker	getting everyone to cooperate and work together
Completer/finisher	working to deadlines and getting jobs completed

Belbin identifies all the positive behaviours that an effective group needs. He also identified 'allowable weaknesses' for each role – if you are good at this, then it's OK to be not so good at that. You can find a self-test version of his questionnaire in earlier editions of his book. Some courses now use his updated commercial version to establish project groups.

Comment

No group of four or five students will have all Belbin's roles represented by different individuals! Each person will have a couple of strong roles and some roles that are not so strong or not preferred.

Belbin argued that a group could adjust its behaviour if it discovered a balance of roles that was not ideal. For example, he describes a group of strong shapers who were not making progress because everyone wanted to lead. The group made time to agree a set of rules and procedures that enabled them to work together.

Hmm...

Think of your own group experience and consider how the different members acted in more or less predictable ways:

▶ Have you noticed that certain people tend to take certain roles?
▶ What were these roles?
▶ To what extent do you think a Belbin-type theory can be useful?

You can also use Belbin's roles as a checklist of things that need to happen in your group, e.g. is the group being coordinated? So you can think about:

▶ Which roles are happening in your group?
▶ Are they all covered?
▶ Are there any gaps? Does it matter? If so, what can you do about it?

∘ O ∘

Schedule regular meetings: agree dates and times at the start of the project.

It can, of course, be difficult to find times to suit everyone, and sometimes groups need to move meeting times around. You need to be flexible, e.g. meeting online to review progress is often easier to organise.

Several technologies can help your group get organised, including:

▶ Scheduling tools to choose the best dates/times.
▶ Meeting planners to confirm times and send out reminders.

Agendas

An agenda sets out what you hope to discuss in a meeting. Ideally, one person (usually the note-taker) will have prepared and distributed this before the meeting. At the beginning of the meeting, ask everyone if they want to add items to it.

Good agendas make sure that you can discuss and record:

▶ progress on the project
▶ what needs to be done next
▶ any problems to be resolved.

The meeting should cover all the items on your agenda. If you run out of time, you can add any items you didn't discuss to the agenda of the next meeting, or decide on an extra meeting to resolve any outstanding issues.

At the end of the meeting, everyone must be clear about what to do next and when actions need to be completed. Your group should decide how these details will be recorded/distributed. For example, you could use Microsoft Teams or Google Docs.

Sample agenda

The following example shows how you can organise your discussion to cover the ideas discussed above. Using a table format gives you space to record decisions and make notes – remember to be clear on who is doing what (and by when). You could also use separate columns for notes and decisions/actions.

Sample agenda

Project meeting agenda Zoom link here		
10am–11am Wednesday 23 November		
	Item	*Notes and decisions/actions*
1	Welcome and introductions	Agree agenda and any extra items
2	Apologies	Who can't attend today?
3	Progress on agreed actions	Need to review everyone's workload
4	Planning for presentation	Need to allocate roles
5	Mike's absence	How do we manage this?
6	Any other business	
7	Actions	What needs doing? By whom? By when?
8	Date and time of next meeting	

Spreading the load

What if some tasks are more demanding than others? There are various things you can do to monitor this – ask members to keep a rough guide of the time they spend on particular tasks. Also, suggest time limits when you divide up and allocate tasks.

Contingency/backup

What if someone is ill? When you allocate tasks, think about nominating a backup person for each task in case of any emergency. Working out which tasks are essential and which are more optional can help you decide how to deal with a crisis.

Online meetings

Many of the concepts above are still relevant. All meetings should have agendas and you need a strategy for recording decisions, actions and progress.

If your group includes students in different countries and time zones, it may not be easy for you to meet at the same time, so most discussions may need to happen over a longer period of time – known as 'asynchronous communication'.

For asynchronous communication, you still need a way of highlighting key decisions and actions so these are clear. Use shared online documents to record:

▶ key decisions made
▶ project aims/targets
▶ actions – who is doing each one and the deadline.

Using the comments feature in documents is a useful way to raise and answer questions. As a result, you can be more certain that everyone has understood and agreed to group activity. This is especially important when the group needs to agree on a new course of action!

Example

A group of Geography students agreed that the presentation needed three main sections, each presented by a different group member. But there were more than three people in the group – what were the others going to do?

The group took time to divide the tasks so that everyone made a significant contribution. For example, one student was really shy and nervous about presenting. The group decided that this person could design the introduction and conclusion slides and set up shared online documents to help the other members design their slide content. Everyone agreed that this seemed fair.

Your group should discuss in the first meeting how you want to make decisions. After a few meetings, review how this is working. You can use tools in social media and chat applications to take polls and/or ask for responses to set questions – a great way to get feedback from each group member.

I vote we aim for consensus!

Our final example illustrates the value of working through disagreement to arrive at a decision that everyone can accept.

Methods

Method	Pros	Cons
Consensus	Everyone is committed to the decision and feels a part of it.	Can take more time. May need a chair who is good at managing discussion.

Method	Pros	Cons
Compromise	Gets the group to a decision.	Does not always resolve underlying issues. May lead to conflict later.
Leader/chair decides	Simple, often quick.	Possible team resentment, risk of poor choice and limited group responsibility.
Vote	Usually considered fair, efficient in 'non-even' groups.	Group may split if there are equal numbers on each side. May lead to problems if there are strong minority opinions.
Pros/cons table	Efficient and can help to clarify a difficult and complicated decision.	Can be time-consuming and choices may still appear quite closely matched.
Random selection	Quick – may help where other methods have failed.	Can result in poor/ ill-informed choices.

Example: the Design students who could not agree

The course contained a week-long practical group project, ending with presentations to the teaching staff team.

One group came to a tutor in the middle of the week, minus one member, saying they had reached an impasse. Jay, the missing member, had a completely different approach to the design and was not willing to budge. The tutor explained that this was not uncommon in design consultancy and the group would have to figure out a way of resolving the disagreement or using it constructively in their presentation. The group went back to Jay and agreed to adopt this second suggestion. Their final presentation discussed both the majority and minority view. Other tutors on the judging panel (all completely unaware of the conflict) decided this was one of the best and most thoughtful presentations. All the group members, including Jay, were satisfied with both process and outcome.

And finally

The best performing groups are well organised. They are clear on who is doing what and by when. They have effective methods to record and monitor their progress using regular meetings, agendas and notes.

Effective decision-making and methods for resolving conflict are also important. However, even the most organised of groups will run into trouble if they don't pay enough attention to how they communicate and maintain group relationships, as we show in Part 4.

RELATIONSHIPS AND COMMUNICATION

Part 4 outlines strategies for keeping your group on track in terms of your relationships and communication. It includes:

▶ analysing what is going on

▶ evidencing everyone's contribution

▶ reviewing and revising your ground rules

▶ dealing with conflict.

Entertainers talk about 'reading' their audience – studying their actions/reactions to decide how they are responding (and adjusting their act accordingly). You can develop skills in 'reading' your group – deciding what is going on, how people are feeling and then determining what you can or should do about it.

Don't we all do this already? Yes, to some extent, but we can get it wrong. Sometimes, groups do not recognise what is going on and sometimes members misinterpret each other. This can be especially true online when we don't have the same body language cues to help us.

Example: the 'democratic' group with the dominant leader

The tutor asked the group how they were getting on. All the members looked at Sam, who immediately responded, saying how well they were doing and how they had decided to 'be democratic with no one leading'. The other members all nodded. This happened every time the tutor asked about progress. The group got stuck later – they did not recognise that they were leaving Sam to decide everything. And then Sam ran out of energy and inspiration …

You may have experienced 'Sam' online! Online groups often have certain keen members who are first to post comments and replies while others post very little at all. The danger is that any group with dominant voices risks missing great ideas and potential issues. In the most effective groups, everybody's voice is heard!

Interpreting your group's behaviour

The following techniques can help you reflect, and help you gain insight into what is going on. They are not intended as activities for you to introduce to the group; they offer an extra dimension to your understanding about your group.

Some tutors use exercises like these in group discussion. They can be very effective but only if the tutor is skilled and experienced and there is enough time. People can develop strong feelings in their group so discussion needs to be carefully managed.

Interaction charts

This is a simple diagram of communication between the group members. It is an 'ideal' group where everyone is communicating positively and equally with everyone else. You are unlikely to find such a group in real life. There will always be some imbalance.

Try making a diagram/interaction chart of your current group. You can use the thickness of lines to suggest the amount or strength of communication between members, as in the next example.

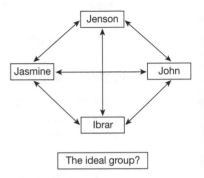

The ideal group?

How would you like to be a member of this group? Here, Duane sends and receives messages from everyone and will probably be seen as the leader. Jo, Aaron and Stella seem to be a bit of a subgroup and Hans seems to be rather isolated. To improve relationships in this group, individuals need to take responsibility in different ways:

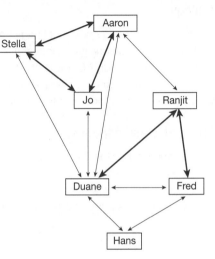

Duane needs to recognise how central he is and try to get everyone equally involved.

Jo, Aaron and Stella need to see how their friendship is excluding others.

Hans needs to consider why he is on the edge of the group. Has he given the impression that he is uninterested or unwilling to join in? Or have the others ignored him because he is a bit shy?

Analogy

Sometimes, an analogy or visual image helps to express an idea. What is your group like? Would you describe it as a jaguar (the animal) – sleek, fast, flexible and fit, but not necessarily very friendly? Or more of a teddy bear – warm and cuddly but a bit slow to do anything? Jaguar groups need to spend more time working on relationships; teddy bear groups need a more urgent approach to the task.

Boundaries and participation

Another approach is to think about the group boundaries. Who is central to the group and who is on the edge? You may discover a boundary within the group so that there are really two subgroups in the room. This can be a problem – subgroups may develop different approaches to group tasks.

Example: boundary problems

In this group, discussion felt to the tutor (and to anyone observing the group from outside) like a table tennis match, with the ball being a comment/idea/suggestion and the two 'players' being the group of younger students on one side and the group of older students sitting on the opposite side of the table.

From individual discussion, the tutor discovered that each subgroup had developed a positive image of itself and a negative image of the others. This is a common pattern in studies of intergroup behaviour.

In this example, the younger students felt intimidated by the older students' confidence. The older students felt intimidated by the younger students' better grasp of academic work. The atmosphere only improved when the tutor introduced ideas and theories of groups and intergroup conflict into their discussion.

Theory box: Positive group behaviour

Researchers have investigated student groups to identify types of behaviour that are associated with positive collaborative outcomes (e.g. Iacob and Faily 2019). Although findings depend on factors like group composition, culture and subject, successful groups usually include:

▸ Fair levels of participation from each person
▸ Respectful communication
▸ Behaviour that suggests a positive mentality towards groupwork.

Where groups don't display these positive behaviours, conflict can occur. Conflict can be quick to develop, and it take lots of time and energy to resolve. It is less likely when groups have established clear ground rules at the start!

What aspects of group behaviour do you notice in your group?
▸ Does your group display the positive behaviours outlined above?
▸ If your group doesn't, how could you encourage this?

▶ If your group has experienced conflict, can you use the theory mentioned above to reflect on why it might have occurred?

° ○ °

Evidencing peer contribution

Ideally, everyone in your group will contribute equally to the project and assessment. Setting up a shared online space will support this and should have been part of your technology map.

You may be asked to complete a peer assessment, using a form that asks every member of the group to rate each student's contribution. Where ratings are inconsistent, the tutor will look at evidence provided in the shared working space and (hopefully) discuss this with the group.

Other examples include peer-moderated marking of groupwork, where students give peers marks against defined criteria and/or are asked to write a reflective account outlining individual contributions.

13 Reviewing and revising your ground rules

In Part 2 we discussed ground rules in two categories:

> communication and attitudes
> working practice.

Agreeing rules does not mean they will automatically work. Review them at least once, ideally halfway through the project, to give you time to change if you need to.

Make sure your ground rules are still useful and relevant. One good way to do this is to turn each of your rules into a question: Are we doing 'X'? (where X is the original ground rule). If you answer 'no', what is the consequence? Does this matter? If it is getting in the way of group progress, then you need to renew or revise the ground rule. The rest of this chapter demonstrates how to approach this.

Communication and attitudes

Effective teams treat everyone with respect and dignity. You can translate this into a personal checklist, as below. The behaviours are ones we identified in our earlier discussion of ground rules. You can ask all group members to complete it. If the answer to any of the questions is 'no', then you need to change – or relationships and communication will go downhill. See the corresponding section below for advice.

Ground rules checklist

Behaviours	Questions to ask yourself include ...	See section ...
Use positive words and body language	Am I making an effort to show enthusiasm? Is my speech polite and at reasonable volume with no words that might offend? Am I facing/looking at my group? Do I show that I am listening to others using body cues like nodding? Online, can I use an emoticon (smiley) to emphasise my comments and convey particular feelings?	A

Give everyone a chance to speak	Am I making enough contribution to discussions? Do I ask others for their thoughts? Do I allow time for people to speak and respond to key points? Do I try to avoid talking for too long or writing really long posts in group chats?	B
Listen and pay attention to each other	Do I make notes and/or acknowledge other people's contributions/ideas verbally? Do I check for understanding by asking questions? Am I able to repeat back/write down someone else's ideas/thoughts in my own words? Online, do I tag other people's comments with reactions so they know what I think?	C
Acknowledge other members' opinions in a balanced, measured way	Do I show that I agree by commenting positively about ideas/thoughts or through body language like nodding/smiling? Am I good at explaining why I agree/disagree? If I don't agree, am I careful to criticise the idea/concept but NOT the person? Do I seem to have a balance of points that I agree or disagree with? Online, I could react using an emoticon – will the meaning be clear? Do I need to explain why I feel that way?	D

A: Positive words and body language

Have you had that experience of feeling happy/relaxed until someone's negative behaviour ruins the mood? It can be uncomfortable, but sometimes we need to stop and listen to what other people are trying to say. You may need to take some time to let someone 'vent': explain how they feel (and why) before the group can move on.

Look for patterns of behaviour that 'add up' to a particular message:

▶ Check consistency between words and body language. Inconsistency is usually important; e.g. the person who says they are 'feeling fine' but their body language looks anxious or distressed.

▶ Look for *changes* in a person's typical body language. Suppose someone regularly uses lots of gestures and hand movements when they talk, and you notice they are suddenly doing this more or less than normal. What does this mean? Is something wrong?

▶ Does someone behave differently online from face-to-face interactions?

▶ Has someone changed the way they post online? Are they suddenly posting a lot less or perhaps using more negative emoticons than usual?

Sometimes, we are the ones behaving in ways that are perceived negatively. For example, we might continue to look at our phone or something else even when someone is talking directly to us. The problem is that we often don't realise how we might be coming across to others.

If you find someone getting annoyed with you or dismissive for any reason, check your own behaviour and be honest if something has upset you. If nothing is wrong, you might be inadvertently sending out the wrong signal. But perhaps you need to talk about an issue that is upsetting you. Either way, negative behaviour can prevent effective group communication.

Microaggressions are particular examples of negative language that can derail a diverse group, especially when the aggressor does not recognise the impact of what they say.

Theory box: Recognising and avoiding microaggressions

As well as research studies, you can find some useful discussions in popular media. For example, Michele Barnwell (2020) introduces both theory and personal experience of being on the receiving end of a microaggression, defining it as 'an indirect, sometimes subtle put-down toward a person from a marginalized community, often wrapped up in what pretends to be a compliment'. She offers ideas on how to avoid delivering a microaggression, such as 'consider what you're about to say by applying it to yourself first'. Many universities now offer practical advice and guidance to help you avoid these issues.

B: Giving everyone a chance to speak

All group members should be given time to speak and contribute, especially in response to a major idea or decision.

In any group there will be confident people and those who are less so. There is always a danger that groups will be dominated, especially in discussions, by strong characters and that shy or nervous members will be ignored or not given enough of an opportunity to voice their thoughts and ideas.

If you are confident, try to encourage other people to get involved wherever possible. Sometimes, they have good ideas but are just too shy to say them. From the other perspective, if you are shy and someone asks for your opinion, try to say what you think – they want to know! It can help to write some thoughts down first so you know what you want to say.

If your usual style of meeting is not working, try another. For some groups, online chats are the best way to communicate and encourage contribution. For other groups, a regular 'live' meeting will be more productive. Experiment a little and find out what works best for your group!

Try:

- allowing 'thinking time' or silence so people can think about the key points
- agreeing a limit for how long one person can talk for
- taking it in turns to speak in a set order; e.g. clockwise round a circle
- asking people what they think in order to encourage participation.

C: Active listening

People often concentrate on what they are going to say next, rather than paying attention to what someone else is saying right now. To be an active listener, you need to:

- understand the message being passed to you
- communicate that you have received and understood the message.

Taking brief notes by writing key words can help if someone has a lot to say. You can then check your understanding by rephrasing and repeating back what they have said or you could ask a question to clarify a key point. Remember your body language!

Try:

summarising what the other person has said in your own words:

- *So, what you are saying is …*
- *OK, so you think that …*
- *Right, you are suggesting that we …*

encouraging the other person nonverbally:

- nod occasionally
- make some eye contact
- ensure that you are facing them.

D: Acknowledging others

Communication is a two-way process. You want to get your message across effectively, of course, but you also need to listen to and understand what other people are trying to tell you.

Sometimes, you can get things wrong. So, you do need to listen to what other people have to say – even if they express it in a way that seems to you to be rude or disrespectful. If someone has upset you, let them know – they may have done it without realising. You also need to make sure that you don't miss the useful part of the message.

At times, it can seem easier to say nothing but if you spot something that the other group members haven't, by discussing it as a group you might solve a looming problem and save yourself from a greater challenge later. It is better to raise your concerns and be proved wrong than to remain silent and be proved right.

Likewise, when you raise a point of view, explain it clearly. It is easy to say that you don't like an idea. It is more useful, however, to say why. In the following example, a student wants to suggest that an idea will prove difficult due to its being too time-consuming. Compare the different ways of expressing this view.

You say ...	Is this the best way to say it?
I don't like your idea.	No, this is a value judgement and is personal.
I'm not sure about that idea.	Better, not personal but a bit vague.
That's one way we could do it, but I think it might be too time-consuming.	Much better. This acknowledges the previous contribution but raises a valid point in a non-personal way.
That's one way we could do it, which would work, but I wonder if it might be too time-consuming. Could we try this instead?	Very good. This acknowledges the previous idea, clearly states your opinion and suggests a possible alternative. It is even more likely to be seen as constructive if your suggestion obviously develops or builds on the other person's proposal.

These suggestions will help you to get away from 'yes, but' thinking, where we immediately think of what might be wrong with someone's suggestion.

Working practice

Is your team making good progress on the task? Revisit your ground rules on this to see if you can identify any areas for improvement.

Keeping in contact

People are busy and will sometimes have to miss meetings – work, family and the unexpected can mean finding a regular time everyone can make really difficult. But do try and establish ways of staying in touch between meetings.

In between meetings, how have you decided to keep in touch? Is this working?

What rules did you establish at the start? Are these rules being maintained? Do they need re-emphasising or renewing?

Can you use technology to help? You might try email, group chat or social media. Most colleges and universities use VLEs with discussion boards – is this the easiest and most accessible answer for your group?

Working practice checklist

If the answer is 'no' for any of these questions, it is probably the group organisation you need to improve (see Part 3 for advice).

Working practice checklist

Original ground rules	Key questions	OK?	If not, go back to this section in Part 3 ...
When and where will we meet?	Are team meetings efficient and organised?		Agendas
Behave professionally	Is everyone turning up? Does everyone communicate if delayed or can't make it? Is everyone doing what they agreed to?		Organising meetings
Will there be team or meeting roles?	If you have team roles, are they working well? If you don't have team roles, do you need them?		Team roles
How will we decide things?	Is your team deciding things effectively? Do you need to change your decision-making method?		Making decisions

14 Dealing with conflict

Sometimes, for a variety of reasons, a group will find itself in conflict. This can upset everyone and may have a severe impact on effective group working. What can you do if this happens to your group?

Theory box: Conflict in groups

One of the most common sources of conflict in student groups is the perception by some group members that others are not contributing enough. Social scientists have known for some time that people can have a tendency to work less hard in group situations, known as 'social loafing', perhaps due to reduced social pressure because responsibility is shared. More recent studies have shown that clear rules about group conduct set at the start of the project and good team communications and clarity on the task (Lam 2015) can help to reduce this effect. So, although social loafing can be a common and significant issue for student groups, there are ways to reduce the risk!

Managing and resolving conflict

When conflict does arise, consider the following four key steps.

1 Open the lines of communication

Professional mediators usually insist on what they call the 'conflict-resolving conversation'. They know the value of making each party sit down around a table and discuss how they might move forward. You need a meeting that *everyone* attends.

2 Define the issues

Do the opposing parties have the same idea about what the issues actually are? Or do they see things very differently?

Try this:

▶ Each person writes down on sticky notes why there is disagreement (one note for each separate comment).
▶ Sticky notes are put on the board or table and the group discussion sorts them into issues to resolve.

Consider: Is it a task-based issue, perhaps a difference of opinion about the best course of action? Or is it a person-centred issue, perhaps a problem relating to reliability or commitment? Can the group continue the project or does this issue need to be resolved before you proceed?

3 Focus on the task

When issues relate to personality clashes or personal difference, people tend to focus more on the issue and less on the task. The technique above should start the group thinking about how to get on with the task. You need to reinforce this in the discussion: if it looks as if personal differences are getting in the way, ask a question or make a comment that will refocus on the task, such as, *We disagree on this but how can we move forward?* Everyone in the group should try to do this.

4 Use your group ground rules

Group conflicts often arise from disagreements about how a group should proceed when several options are on the table. You should have committed to certain ways of deciding things in your original ground rules. Go back to the rules and review them again. If you are still stuck or can't work things out, seek help from your tutor.

Hmm...

Conflict resolution is a major area of international research and study. There are plenty of websites with tips on how to resolve group conflict. See if you can find any that might help you reflect on your own situation and add further tips to the ones above.

Example: the group with the 'missing' member

The group struggled to get any responses from one group member. They could not get him to turn up to meetings. Finally, they mentioned this to their tutor. He advised them to:

- continue working together without the missing member
- keep a clear record of attendance and contribution
- plan what they might allow him to do if he decided to get back in touch (perhaps contribute some slides or do a bit of the presentation).

The tutor reminded them that it would be clear from the individual assignment who had not contributed to their group and that there were marks from peer assessment. This demonstrates that you need a backup plan if conflict resolution fails.

Hmm...

Think about any past conflicts you have been involved in that you managed to solve:

▶ How did you resolve the conflict?
▶ Do you think you were able to think rationally at the time?
▶ What did you learn from the experience?

And finally

Successful groups take time to listen to each other and each group member works to stay engaged with every other member of the group. In great teams, discussions are open and honest: the team is able to deal with disagreements in a respectful and effective way. Dealing with problems and disagreements is a vital part of effective group working and we learn by reflecting on our mistakes as well as our successes. One of the most important skills you can develop to help you improve your group performance is reflection, as we suggest in Part 5.

Part 5 will help you to:

▶ check you have met the demands of the current assignment

▶ reflect on your experience of groupwork

▶ write this reflection up for an assignment

▶ use your experience to do things better next time.

Our troubleshooting guide summarises the main ideas from this book.

On pages 40–46 we emphasised the importance of working out what the assignment was about. What counts as good performance?

Below we consider the group presentation that concludes many projects. You can apply similar questions to whatever 'product' your project has to deliver.

Delivering an effective presentation

Use this checklist to make sure you have all the necessary information. The notes suggest some issues you need to sort out.

Presentation checklist

Key question	Notes
Where/how will the presentation take place?	Visit this room beforehand and get to know it. Ideally, book a rehearsal. If your presentation is online, rehearse it using the technology you will use on the day. Decide how to share screens and change speakers if you have more than one presenter.

Key question	Notes
How long do we have?	Keep to time. Many tutors cut you off at the allotted time regardless of whether you have finished. Ask the tutor for a 'one minute warning' so you can summarise at the end.
Who is the audience?	Will your tutor be listening/questioning from a particular perspective or role? Will other student groups or other people be there? If the audience is online, how will they be able to participate?
What facilities will we have? *What is the expected format?*	PowerPoint is commonplace but what about alternatives? What if the tutor excludes PowerPoint? (Some tutors do this to force you to consider alternative approaches.) Are you expected to produce a handout? If you are online, then other details need checking. For example, are you expected to use/respond to comments in the chat box? Will all your slides 'work' as you expect online?
What is its purpose?	For example, are you being asked to summarise all the work you have done or just present main conclusions and implications? Do you have to relate what you have done to work elsewhere, perhaps major theories or industrial practice?

Key question	Notes
What is the best way of achieving this?	Is a conventional PowerPoint the best way to put your message across?
Who has to present?	Does everyone have to take a turn and say a bit? If not, how will you organise the group while the presentation is going on?

More detail on creating and delivering effective presentations can be found in *Posters and Presentations* in this series.

Examples

Integrating different methods into your presentations

Student groups sometimes do not bring enough variety into their presentations. For example, one group that kept their tutor's attention used:

▶ opening quiz (from Kahoot!) to introduce main issues
▶ PowerPoint to summarise key points
▶ video of group's roleplay to illustrate practical implications
▶ brief discussion exercise for everyone in the audience
▶ responses to questions from the audience.

The presentation was well rehearsed and achieved excellent marks.

The Business students who flunked the game

Student groups played a business game to prepare for their written assessment. They made regular decisions to build a profitable business, trying to 'beat' the computer.

After a few bad decisions, one group realised they had no chance of winning the game. They concentrated on working out the assumptions behind the game, reasoning that this would give them a head start on the assignment. They were right. This group understood the rules of the game better than the group who 'won', achieving excellent marks in the assignment.

By reflecting on what they really needed to learn, this group turned the game into effective preparation for their assessment.

What makes 'good' reflection?

Reflection is a powerful tool for learning from experience and doing better next time.

Being open to feedback

Accepting the need to improve is not always easy. The first step is recognising feedback as a vital and useful part of self-development. We only use it fully if we are open to the information.

Do you need more information?

To use feedback – from tutors or other students – you need to understand it. If feedback is not completely clear, contact the provider and seek clarification.

Theory box: Intercultural groupwork

For modern workplaces, you need good intercultural skills – the ability to work effectively with people from different cultures/places. Many universities provide opportunities to develop these skills through collaborative online international learning (COIL) or virtual exchange programmes. These involve students working online in groups with learners from other countries. Students develop intercultural competences in three key areas.

Knowledge (*knowing*)	Skills (*doing*)	Attributes (*being*)
Cultural self-awareness Facts about other cultures Global trends/issues	Listening Communicating with respect Critical thinking Reflection	Openness Curiosity Respect for value of difference/humility Resilience for challenge

This table adapts ideas from Darla Deardorff's (2006) process model of intercultural competence to summarise qualities for effective intercultural collaboration.

> *Hmm...*
>
> If your groupwork involved cross-cultural collaboration, you can use these ideas to reflect on:
>
> ▸ What did you learn about another culture?
> ▸ How have your communication skills improved?
> ▸ What have you learned about yourself?

Five-step reflection model

Many students are confused by what tutors want from reflection. As a starting point, you can satisfy most tutors if you answer the following five questions:

1 *What did you and the group do well?*
Recognise the aspects of your work you completed well. This should include anything you know went well or you have received praise for. Make sure you understand why it was viewed positively.

2 How did you feel about your progress?

Think about how you felt during the progress.

Don't ignore any feelings as these are important clues about the group progress.

Do you now feel more confident or do you need to be more assertive?

3 What could be improved?

Identify feedback that suggests room for improvement.

4 How can you explain what worked and what did not?

Most tutors want you to relate your experience to general principles and theory to show that you have deepened your understanding.

5 How would you do things differently next time?

Suggest possible actions you can take to improve your performance next time.

The following template gives you a structure for reflecting on an event or situation – an example is provided.

Reflection template

Event (include date and time)	14 November, 2.00–3.30 Meeting to try out the presentation for the first time
What happened?	We all arrived on time except for Jed, so didn't start till after he arrived at 2.15. Nobody questioned or challenged Jed on his lateness. We did two run-throughs with all the PowerPoint slides and then discussed them to see where we could improve. Jasmine looked upset when Jed criticised her slides. We changed a few slides for the second run-through. We agreed a meeting before the formal presentation to have a final run-through.
How did you feel?	I felt frustrated we started late; it did not give us enough time to review our first run-through as thoroughly as I would have liked. I felt sorry for Jasmine as Jed was overcritical.
What went well?	Our overall argument came across clearer in the second run-through.
What could be improved?	Jed's late arrival with no explanation created tension. Our timing is a bit wrong as we are still two minutes over. We have not got a strategy to fix this.

Event (include date and time)	14 November, 2.00–3.30 Meeting to try out the presentation for the first time
How can you explain what worked and what did not?	We have not become a well-organised 'team' if you look at the theories. We never discussed critical issues; e.g. leadership and group organisation. We accepted Jed as leader because of his self-confidence, but he does not seem to want to live up to our expectations.
What have you learned/could do differently next time?	We did not have a contingency plan for anyone arriving late: What if this happened on the day? We had a ground rule of 'supportive criticism' – Jed did not follow this. I should be more supportive.

For more on reflective writing and how to approach it see *Reflective Writing* in this series.

SWOT analysis

This is a way of reflecting on your strengths, weaknesses, opportunities and threats. You can analyse your groupwork skills and/or your contribution. This example suggests what it might look like.

Strengths *What are your most confident skills?* **Problem solving**: I enjoy researching new ways to find solutions.	Weaknesses *Which skills do you feel you need to improve?* **Presenting**: Not as confident at presenting as other members. Must practise communication skills by rehearsing more.
Opportunities *What did you contribute to the group?* **Creativity**: Was first to suggest concept mapping to brainstorm ideas and was able to help others use it.	Threats *What issues impeded you?* **Time management**: Need to be better organised. Without a to-do list and personal deadlines, I let myself and the group down.

If you have made notes on important events in your group's history, you will have plenty of material.

Two things can help you decide what should go into the assignment:

- What issues or themes have cropped up regularly? (The examples above demonstrate issues of coordination and leadership.)
- How does your experience of the group compare with generally accepted ideas and theories about group behaviour?

The theory box gives you one example comparison.

Theory box: Models of group development

Theory

Perhaps the best-known theory with regard to group development was devised by Bruce Tuckman (see Hartley 1997), based on a review of previous studies. His four stages are often cited as the definitive model.

Tuckman suggested that most groups go through a series of recognisable stages during the course of a project. These are:

Forming There is uncertainty and insecurity, as group members get to know one another and work out how they might work together.

Storming Conflict and disagreement surface as group members become more confident and comfortable in airing their opinions. Power struggles and cliques may develop.

Norming Consensus emerges as the group finds effective ways both to get on with each other and work together efficiently.

Performing The group becomes effective, with a clear, shared view of the task and a settled way of working.

Adjourning (fifth stage, added later) The group prepares to split up. There can be feelings of satisfaction but also sadness and loss.

Comment

Always identify possible limitations in theories. For example, Tuckman based his model on studies from the 1960s and 70s and did not focus on student groups.

Look for alternative models/explanations. For example, some studies of student groups use 'punctuated equilibrium' theory – the group sets off quickly but hits a 'crisis point' halfway through, which it has to resolve before carrying on (Gersick 2019). This theory explains some of the groups we have worked with and is why we always recommend a 'review meeting' halfway through every project.

Tuckman offers a useful starting point to review your group process. How far did your group follow this pattern? Don't worry if your group did not! One student group apologised that they 'didn't seem to be doing it right as they had not stormed'. The tutor explained that this is *only one model* of how groups behave. This group avoided storming by being very well organised and cooperative from the start.

Action planning

Using feedback from tutors, set targets to improve. Try to express these in ways that make them easier to achieve, i.e. SMART targets are specific, measurable, achievable, realistic and timely.

If the tutor criticised the 'overlong and woolly' introduction at your last presentation, turn this into targets for next time.

Targets checklist

	Check ✔
Is my target/goal specific enough?	Aim to get good feedback on my next introduction
Is my goal measurable?	Will ask tutor for specific measures
Is my goal achievable?	Yes
Is my goal realistic?	I'll research ideas/examples of good presentations and volunteer to do the introduction next time
Is my goal time-bound (date for completion)?	Next presentation is in four weeks

Hmm...

And a final Hmm ...

Think about your groupwork experience and what you have learned:

▶ What did you do well?
▶ What could you have improved?
▶ What have you learned from the experience and/or this book?
▶ What might you do differently next time in a group?

And finally

Working in groups can develop your abilities to:

▶ Learn about other people and create teams.
▶ Collaboratively interpret a task and decide how to achieve it as a team.
▶ Organise with others to make the best of everyone's knowledge and skills.
▶ Communicate effectively and manage relationships to get the most from teamwork.
▶ Reflect on areas for development so you can improve next time.

Chapter 1 listed questions that employers often ask to assess how well you work in teams. After each project, try to answer them. Consider keeping your answers in a document to update/revise. This makes a great reference tool for interviews to help you demonstrate your expertise in groupwork!

We wish you good fortune in all your current and future groupwork.

Troubleshooting guide

Issue	Suggestions
Don't know where to start	• Start with introductions and maybe a discussion of group members' skills/interests. • Discuss and decide on your ground rules. • Discuss what technologies you can use to support the project, e.g. where/how are you going to store any documents? How is the group going to stay in touch? • Get everyone to read a copy of the assignment instructions and the marking criteria. Give everyone five minutes to come up with initial thoughts – share with group. Do this as a 'brainstorming' exercise where you list all the thoughts and then discuss/evaluate them. • Ask if anyone in the group has done this type of project before. Invite them to talk about how it went and what they learned from it.
Don't know how to get organised	• Meet regularly! • Decide on a mix of face-to-face and online meetings – use face to face to agree the plan and make major decisions; use regular short online meetings to check progress. • Create a plan that everyone agrees and is kept up to date. • Decide on your final product/output. Work backwards from the hand-in date and think of all the stages you need to complete and how long you need for each.

Issue	Suggestions
	<ul><li>Break the plan into 'mini-tasks' and allocate these to group members with targets for completion.</li><li>Record who is doing what.</li><li>Discuss your plan and progress in each meeting.</li></ul>
Can't decide what to do	<ul><li>Write all your options down.</li><li>Draw up a list of pros and cons.</li><li>Choose the top two options.</li><li>Take a vote on the best option.</li><li>Move on.</li></ul>
Group conflict	<ul><li>Get each group member to write down what they think the problem is (can be done anonymously on a Padlet). Give everyone time to read all the comments and then get the group to sit down together and discuss.</li><li>Focus on moving forward with the task.</li><li>Emphasise how successful completion will benefit every group member.</li><li>Focus on the project actions and ignore any personal differences. Decide what needs to be completed to finish the project.</li><li>If all else fails, contact tutor.</li></ul>
Non-participation	<ul><li>Agree at the start what action you will take if this happens.</li><li>Attempt to contact the person and ask them to explain why they are not engaging and what they suggest you do. Explain what will happen if you don't hear from them.</li><li>Keep clear records of meetings and attendance and make sure there is a record of who has done what.</li></ul>

Issue	Suggestions
	• Reallocate any work you need to and complete the project without the missing member.
	• Have a plan if they re-engage – is there anything you could give them to do?
	• Inform tutor of your situation as soon as it is obvious there is a problem.
	• Keep your tutor up to date on how it develops.

References

Azad N, Anderson HG Jr, Brooks A et al. (2017) Leadership and management are one and the same. *American Journal of Pharmaceutical Education*, 81(6): 102. doi:10.5688/ajpe816102.

Bailenson JN (2021) Nonverbal Overload: A theoretical argument for the causes of Zoom fatigue. *Technology, Mind, and Behavior*, 2(1). https://doi.org/10.1037/tmb0000030.

Barnwell M (2020) Why it's so important to understand and confront microaggressions. *Good Housekeeping*, 4 August. Available at www.good_housekeeping.com/life/a33404079/what-are-microaggressions/.

Beeson H (2021) *Groupwork: Common issues*. https://mypad.northampton.ac.uk/groupworkskills/.

Beeson H and Byles R (2020) Creative solutions to common groupwork problems. *Journal of Learning Development in Higher Education*,19. https://doi.org/10.47408/jldhe.vi19.622.

Belbin RM (2010) *Management Teams: Why they succeed or fail* (3rd edn). Oxford: Butterworth Heinemann.

Bethell E and Milsom C (2014) *Posters and Presentations*. London: Red Globe Press.

Chiocchio F and Essiembre H (2009) Cohesion and Performance: A meta-analytic review of disparities between project teams, production teams, and service teams. *Small Group Research*, 40(4): 382–420.

Coding Tech (2018) *Secrets of successful teamwork: Insights from Google.* www.youtube.com/watch?v=hHIikHJV9fI.

Coyle D (2018) *The Culture Code: The secrets of highly successful groups*. London: Random House.

Deardorff DK (2006) The identification and assessment of intercultural competence as a student outcome of internationalization at institutions of higher education in the United States. *Journal of Studies in International Education*, 10(3): 241–66.

Gersick CJ (2019) Reflections on revolutionary change. *Journal of Change Management*, DOI: 10.1080/14697017.2019.1586362.

Hartley P (1997) *Group Communication*. London: Routledge.

Harvard Business School (2004) *Teams that Click*. Boston: Harvard Business School Press.

Iacob C and Faily S (2019) Exploring the gap between the student expectations and the reality of teamwork in undergraduate software engineering group projects. *Journal of Systems and Software*, 157, 110393. https://doi.org/10.1016/j.jss.2019.110393.

Institute of Student Employers (2018) *The global skills gap in the 21st century*. Report for ISE Members. https://ise.org.uk/page/ISEPublications.

Kolb DA (1984) *Experiential learning: Experience as the source of learning and development*. Upper Saddle River, NJ: Prentice Hall.

Lam C (2015) The role of communication and cohesion in reducing social loafing in group projects. *Business and Professional Communication Quarterly*, 78(4): 454–75.

Leskinen J, Kumpulainen K, Kajamaa A. et al. (2020) The emergence of leadership in students' group interaction in a school-based makerspace. *European Journal of Psychology of Education*. https://doi.org/10.1007/s10212-020-00509-x.

Seethamraju R and Borman M (2009) Influence of group formation choices on academic performance. *Assessment and Evaluation in Higher Education*, 34(1): 31–40.

Syed M (2019) *Rebel Ideas: The power of diverse thinking*. London: John Murray.

West M (2012) *Effective Teamwork* (3rd edn). Oxford: BPS Blackwell.

Wheelan SA (2009) Group size, group development, and group productivity. *Small Group Research*, 40(2): 247–62.

Williams K, Woolliams M and Spiro J (2020) *Reflective Writing* (2nd edn). London: Red Globe Press.

Index

Action plan 112
Active listening 87
Agendas 63, 64
Assessment/criteria 43, 44, 46, 97, 98
Assignments x, 4, 15, 40–42, 100, 101
    Checklist 43–45
Asynchronous communication 66
Attitudes 80
Audience 41, 43, 45, 72

Belbin team roles 58–61
Body language 83
Brainstorm 47

Cognitive diversity 4
Communication 8, 9, 10, 13, 16, 17, 32, 33,
        80, 85, 88
    Online 35, 36, 86
Concept map/mapping 30, 48
Conflict 20, 92
Conflict resolution 93–96

Consensus 67

Decision making 67–70

Emoticon 81, 82
Expectations 8
Experiential learning 5
    Kolb's model 5, 6

Google/Google Docs 12, 15, 28, 63
Ground rules 19, 32–34, 37, 80
Group boundaries 76–77
Group development 110–111
Group selection 19, 20–23
Groupwork checklist 3

Hierarchy 15

Inclusive/inclusivity 16, 17
Interaction chart 74–75
Interviews 2

Intercultural groupwork 103–104

Key issues 11

Leadership 54, 55, 72
LearnHigher vii

Management 54
Meetings 19, 24, 26, 50, 51, 62, 90
    Online 26, 27, 65
Microaggression 32, 85
Microsoft Teams 30
Milestones 48, 63

Organisation 10, 17

Padlet 47
Peer assessment 79
Plan/planning 17, 31, 37, 49, 50
Positive behaviour 25, 78, 81, 83
Presentations 42
    Checklist 98–100

Reality checklist 52
Reflection x, 13, 15, 17, 96, 97, 102, 108

Model 104–105
    Template 106–107
Research 14, 22, 23, 31, 42, 44

Skills viii, ix, 2, 25
Social loafing 92
Social science 4
Social sensitivity 16
Success (factors) 12, 14, 15, 16, 22
SWOT analysis 108

Teams 13, 19
Team reflexivity 14
Team/group roles 53, 56, 57, 58
Technology Map 29–31
Trello 47

Understanding tasks 40–42

VLE 29, 30

Working practice 32, 33, 80, 90, 91
Workload 10, 51

Zoom fatigue 36